The Art of the New American Nation

by **Shirley Glubok**   Designed by Gerard Nook

Early 19th century,
pine wood, gilded,
The Metropolitan Museum
of Art, Purchase, 1959,
The Ella Morris de Peyster Bequest

MACMILLAN PUBLISHING CO., INC.

NEW YORK

COLLIER MACMILLAN PUBLISHERS

LONDON

The author gratefully acknowledges the kind assistance of: *Milton W. Brown*, Professor of Art History, Graduate Division, City University of New York; *Catherine Lynn Frangiamore*, Assistant Curator of Decorative Arts, The Cooper-Hewitt Museum of Decorative Arts and Design; *Mary C. Glaze*, Associate Curator of the American Wing, The Metropolitan Museum of Art; *John K. Howat*, Associate Curator in charge of American Paintings and Sculpture, The Metropolitan Museum of Art; *Ellen Malino James*, Lecturer in American History, The New School of Social Research; *Agnes Halsey Jones*; *Emma M. Papert*, Senior Librarian, The Metropolitan Museum of Art; *Philip F. Purrington*, Curator, Old Dartmouth Historical Society Whaling Museum; *Natalie Spassky*, Curatorial Assistant, American Paintings and Sculpture, The Metropolitan Museum of Art; *Lynn Breidenbach* and *Christopher Pope*; and especially the helpful assistance of *Jay E. Cantor*.

Other books by Shirley Glubok:
THE ART OF ANCIENT EGYPT
THE ART OF LANDS IN THE BIBLE
THE ART OF ANCIENT GREECE
THE ART OF THE NORTH AMERICAN INDIAN
THE ART OF THE ESKIMO
THE ART OF ANCIENT ROME
THE ART OF AFRICA
ART AND ARCHAEOLOGY
THE ART OF ANCIENT PERU
THE ART OF THE ETRUSCANS
THE ART OF ANCIENT MEXICO
KNIGHTS IN ARMOR
THE ART OF INDIA
THE ART OF JAPAN
THE ART OF COLONIAL AMERICA
THE ART OF THE SOUTHWEST INDIANS
THE ART OF THE OLD WEST
THE FALL OF THE AZTECS
THE FALL OF THE INCAS
DISCOVERING TUT-ANKH-AMEN'S TOMB
DISCOVERING THE ROYAL TOMBS AT UR
DIGGING IN ASSYRIA
HOME AND CHILD LIFE IN COLONIAL DAYS

Front cover illustration: *The Sargent Family*, artist unknown, 1800, oil, National Gallery of Art, Collection of Edgar William and Bernice Chrysler Garbisch
Back cover illustration: *Great Blue Heron* by John James Audubon, 1821, watercolor, The New-York Historical Society

Lady with Her Pets
by Rufus Hathaway, 1790, oil,
The Metropolitan Museum of Art,
Gift of Edgar William and
Bernice Chrysler Garbish, 1963

The adoption of the Declaration of Independence on July 4, 1776, began the transformation of thirteen English colonies into one American nation. In its first fifty years the new United States survived two wars with England (the Revolutionary War and the War of 1812), battles with pirates from North Africa and quarrels with France and Spain.

In spite of all difficulties the new nation grew stronger. It tried out new forms of government and developed new forms of art. The early years after the Revolutionary War are known as the Federal period.

One of the earliest engagements of the Revolutionary War, the Battle of Bunker's Hill, was fought near Boston, Massachusetts, on June 17, 1775. The British had attacked the Massachusetts patriots on hills overlooking Boston Harbor. A thousand redcoats were killed or wounded before the patriots were driven from the hills. Soon afterward, George Washington came to Boston to take command of the American troops.

This painting of the battle is by John Trumbull, son of a Connecticut governor and an aide to General Washington during the first year of the Revolution. Later he went to London to study painting with Benjamin West, the first American artist to become internationally known. Trumbull made a series of paintings which became a historical record of the Revolutionary War.

1786, oil, Yale University Art Gallery

*Washington at
Verplanck's Point,*
1790, oil,
The Henry Francis
du Pont
Winterthur Museum

6

Trumbull's portrait of Washington as commander in chief of the Continental army shows the general with his troops and the Hudson River in the background.

Some of the first ships to fly the American flag were seized by pirates who operated out of the Barbary coast of North Africa. To put down the pirates the United States constructed the battleship *Philadelphia,* as illustrated in this engraving by William Russell Birch. An engraving is made by cutting lines into a metal plate. The grooves are filled with ink, then paper is pressed against the plate. Thus the drawing is transferred to the paper.

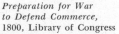

Preparation for War to Defend Commerce, 1800, Library of Congress

Charles Willson Peale was the leading figure of the first important family of artists in early America. He started out in life as a saddler, and became a skillful watchmaker, sign painter, silversmith, dentist, farmer and a soldier in the Revolutionary War. Peale painted portraits of most of the important people of the period, including George Washington, Benjamin Franklin and Thomas Jefferson. Later he founded the first scientific museum in the country, in Philadelphia. Before he died at eighty-six, he had become a naturalist, archaeologist and inventor.

When bones of a mastodon, a gigantic prehistoric animal, were discovered in a marshy pit in the Hudson valley in New York State, Peale arranged to take over the excavation, or dig. With the bones that were dug up he succeeded in reconstructing two skeletons. This painting by Peale shows the dig in progress. Visitors and workers are all very busy. The artist is shown with his family at the far right. He is holding a large drawing of a mastodon bone.

Peale invented the machine which is removing water from the muddy pits. A chain of buckets was raised and lowered by the revolving of the huge wheel. This wheel was turned by people, walking inside it, whose steps made it move.

Exhuming the Mastodon, 1806–1808, oil,
The Peale Museum, Baltimore, Gift of
Mrs. Harry White in memory of her husband

Staircase Group, 1795, oil,
Philadelphia Museum of Art,
The George W. Elkins Collection

Peale named his first four sons, Titian, Raphaelle, Rembrandt and Rubens, after famous European artists. This life-size double portrait of Titian and Raphaelle Peale was painted by their father. The boys are on a flight of stairs, where they seem to have stopped suddenly to look around. Raphaelle is holding an artist's palette and a brush. The painting was first exhibited inside the frame of a real doorway with a wooden step placed in front of it. The painting looked so real that it was said to have fooled George Washington, who nodded politely to the boys as he passed by.

Rembrandt Peale painted his brother Rubens next to a geranium plant. This plant may have been the first geranium in America. It was exhibited in Baltimore at the art and science museum which Rembrandt Peale had founded. The painting is both a portrait and a still life. A still life is a picture of an object or a group of objects, such as flowers, fruit and dishes, artistically arranged.

1801, oil, Collection of Mrs. Norman B. Woolworth

When the Connecticut artist Ralph Earl painted portraits, he filled in the background with details of the lives of the persons he was painting. Below are Oliver Ellsworth and his wife. Earl painted them dressed in fine clothes, seated inside their home. At the same time he showed the exterior, or outside, of their house

1792, oil, Wadsworth Atheneum, Hartford

1796, oil, Museum of Fine Arts, Boston, Purchased by
Washington Association Boston; Boston Athenaeum 1831

as if it were being seen through a window. Ellsworth was a senator from Connecticut

and a chief justice of the United States. He helped to frame the United States

Constitution, which is shown in his hand.

The most famous portrait of George Washington, the first president of the

United States, is by Gilbert Stuart, an artist who grew up in Newport, Rhode Island.

He also painted the companion portrait of Washington's wife, Martha. Stuart used

a simple background in order not to distract attention from the faces of his subjects.

Stuart never finished these portraits; he used them to make about seventy-five copies,

which he sold. This is the portrait of Washington that appears on the face of the

United States' one-dollar bill.

In the early years of the United States artists chose as subjects people, historical events or scenes of daily life, which they painted realistically. Washington Allston was one of the first American artists to find subjects for his paintings in his own imagination. He created pictures of magical beauty filled with poetic mood.

The Rising of a Thunderstorm at Sea illustrates man's never-ending struggle with the terrifying powers of nature. The crew of the small boat frantically lowers the sails as a storm comes up and the wind whips the sea into huge waves. Dark clouds are rapidly covering the sun and sky. The tiny humans in the little boat seem lost and lonely in the vast expanse of ocean.

Allston was born in South Carolina, but spent most of his life in Boston. He studied art in London with Benjamin West, who was friend and teacher to many young American painters. Allston was one of the first Americans to study art in Paris and Rome as well.

1804, oil, Museum of Fine Arts, Boston, Purchased from Everett Fund

Constructed 1803–1812, aquatint by W. G. Wall, 1826, engraved and colored by I. Hill,
Museum of the City of New York, The J. Clarence Davies Collection

Some of the finest public buildings in America were constructed during the

Federal period. Above is an old print of the New York City Hall, made soon after

it was completed. The building was designed by John McComb, Jr., and the French

architect and engineer Joseph François Mangin. It is constructed of smooth stone and

is two stories high. The central section has a grand flight of stairs leading up to an

open porch. On top of the roof is a cupola, a small structure which appeared on most

public buildings.

A leading architect in New England, Charles Bulfinch, designed the state capitols of Massachusetts, Connecticut and Maine. Below is a photograph of the Massachusetts State Capitol in Boston. The brick building is crowned by a dome, on top of which is a cupola. The dome, originally of wood, was later covered with copper by Paul Revere's foundry. Today it is covered with gold leaf, thin sheets of bright gold.

1795–1798, photograph by Alfred Tamarin

In the Federal period ancient Greek and Roman models were used to develop new forms of art. Interest in classical Greece and Rome was growing because ancient monuments, which had long been buried, were being uncovered. The design for the United States Capitol building in the new city of Washington, D.C., was inspired by Roman temples. It was designed by a physician and amateur architect, Dr. William Thornton. George Washington laid the cornerstone in 1793. Benjamin Latrobe was one of several architects who supervised the construction.

When the British occupied Washington during the War of 1812, they set fire to the unfinished Capitol building, but the structure was saved by a heavy rainstorm and

(Detail) by Charles Burton, 1824, The Metropolitan Museum of Art, Purchase, 1942, Joseph Pulitzer Bequest

1822, oil, The Corcoran Gallery of Art, Washington, D.C.

quick action by a small group of American patriots. The Boston architect Bulfinch

completed the building in 1824, when the watercolor at left was made. The streets of

Washington had not yet been paved and the trees were newly planted.

This view of the old House of Representatives in the Capitol was painted by

Samuel F. B. Morse. The artist reproduced the interior architecture and made eighty-six

individual portrait studies. Morse was one of the first Americans to become interested

in photography. He is famous for inventing the telegraph and creating the Morse

code, an alphabet of dots and dashes used for signaling.

Robert Fulton, the inventor of the steamboat,
was also an outstanding artist. He painted the
portrait below in watercolor on ivory. It is a
miniature, a tiny portrait, only three and a half
inches high.

Thomas Sully completed more than 2,500
portraits during his lifetime. He painted his nine-
year-old son Tom in ordinary clothes and a torn
hat. Sully, like so many American artists of his
day, studied in England.

John Vanderlyn was an American
artist who studied in France. In the painting
at right, Vanderlyn placed mother and
child in a classical setting. In this and the
Fulton miniature portrait the dresses and
hair styles are modeled after ancient Greek
and Roman fashions.

1816, oil, Art Commission of the City of New York

John Wesley Jarvis painted a series of full-length portraits of outstanding American military and naval figures of the War of 1812. They were made to hang in the Governor's Room of New York City Hall. One of the war heroes was young Captain Oliver Hazard Perry.

At left Jarvis captures a dramatic moment during the Battle of Lake Erie. The heroic Perry is being transferred from a disabled battleship. He stands surrounded by three sailors, bravely steering a small boat. Perry managed to reach another battleship, the *Niagara,* and win a victory over the British. The sailor in the striped shirt and tall hat is said to be a likeness of the painter, Jarvis.

Engraved by Benzamin Tanner, 1814,
The Metropolitan Museum of Art, Rogers Fund, 1919

Another American victory in the War of 1812 was won when the battleship

United States defeated the British *Macedonian*. This engagement is shown

in an engraving made from a painting by Thomas Birch, who was known for

his marine scenes. Thomas was the son of William Russell Birch the engraver.

1821, oil, National Collection of Fine Arts,
Smithsonian Institution, Gift of Miss Helen Barlow

Early in the nineteenth century many Western Indians were invited to the

city of Washington for conferences and to make peace treaties with the new

nation. They were often taken on grand tours of the important Eastern cities.

Charles Bird King, a popular portrait painter in Washington, was fascinated by the Indian visitors. At left is a King group, *Young Omawhaw, War Eagle, Little Missouri and Pawnees*. These five warriors were presented to President James Monroe. Then they painted their faces and performed a war dance for him. Around the neck of War Eagle is a medal given to him by the President.

The earliest of these Plains Indian visitors to Washington were received by President Thomas Jefferson. Charles B. J. F. de Saint-Mémin, a well-known portrait painter in the East, made this watercolor of a young warrior of the Osage tribe, wearing face paint and long ear pipes. His headdress and ornaments show the Indian before his dress and customs were changed by contact with white men.

Saint-Mémin often used a mechanical instrument called a physiognotrace to make sketches of his subjects. With this device he traced a life-size profile. Then he colored the sketch.

1804, The Henry
Francis du Pont
Winterthur Museum

This painting by Mather Brown is the earliest known portrait of Thomas Jefferson, third president of the United States. It was made in 1786 when the young statesman was United States Ambassador to France. The paper scroll on the table is a reminder that Jefferson was a literary man, whose writings included the Declaration of Independence.

1786, oil,
Collection of
Charles Francis Adams,
photograph Frick Art
Reference Library

1770–1809, photograph by Wayne Andrews

Brown painted this portrait of Jefferson for John Adams, who became the second president of the United States. Both Adams and Jefferson died on July 4, 1826, exactly fifty years after the adoption of the Declaration of Independence.

Jefferson was very much interested in architecture. He played an important role in choosing the architects for the United States Capitol building in Washington. Jefferson designed the State Capitol of Virginia and planned the buildings at the University of Virginia, which he founded. He also designed Monticello, above, his home near Charlottesville, Virginia. It is a three-storied brick building with thirty-five rooms. In the center is a tall porch with six columns in the Greek style. The low dome is modeled after Roman temples.

Nathaniel Russell House, before 1809,
photograph Historic Charleston Foundation

One of the most elegant residences in the South is this brick house in Charleston, South Carolina. The style of architecture is called Adam after the architects Robert and James Adam, two brothers who worked in London. The three-storied building stands behind a low brick wall. The odd-shaped extension at the left accommodates large oval rooms, one on each floor.

At right is a graceful stair hall from Montmorenci, a North Carolina mansion. The sweeping spiral staircase is free-hanging: it seems to float, without side supports so that one can walk underneath and around it.

The chairs and settees, or wide seats, as well as the sewing table, were made by John Seymour and his son Thomas, English-trained cabinetmakers. The sewing table, standing between two chairs, has a hanging sack of pleated silk to hold needles and thread. The rugs were imported from Persia. The punch bowls and urns are from China, reflecting the growing China trade.

Montmorenci, 1822, The Henry Francis du Pont Winterthur Museum

Peirce-Nichols House, 1782, photograph by Alfred Tamarin

A major port for America's ocean-going trade was the seacoast town of Salem, Massachusetts. There wealthy merchants built splendid houses. This large three-storied wooden house was designed by Samuel McIntire, an architect, designer, cabinetmaker and wood carver.

At the gateway are two wooden pillars with carved vases on top. Over the front doorway is a triangular pediment, and at the corners of the house are pilasters, or attached columns, extending the full height of the building. On the edge of the roof is a balustrade, and above that is another railing enclosing a captain's walk.

The house has beautiful wood carvings both inside and out. McIntire himself is said to have carved some of these decorations.

William Rush was one of the first professional sculptors in America. He began his career carving ships' figureheads, which were symbols of the ship, thought to bring good luck. The wooden likeness of Benjamin Franklin below once decorated the prow of a ship. It was brightly painted when new.

Carved wooden statues were often used as signs in front of stores. The figure at right is from a shop where ships' navigating instruments were sold. It was probably made in Newport, Rhode Island, another of New England's major seaports.

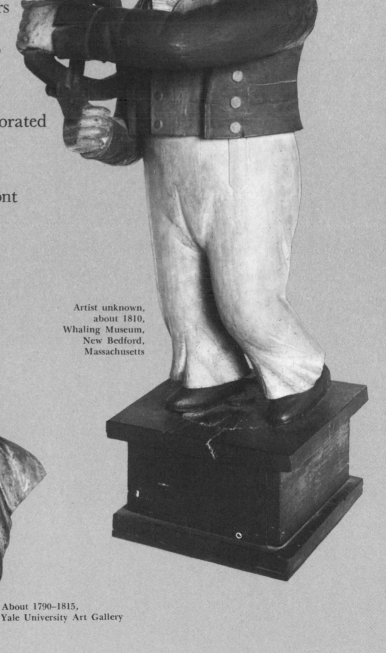

Artist unknown,
about 1810,
Whaling Museum,
New Bedford,
Massachusetts

About 1790–1815,
Yale University Art Gallery

31

About 1820, The Metropolitan Museum of Art, Rogers Fund, 1922

One of the best-known cabinetmakers in America was the Scotsman Duncan

Phyfe. Phyfe's furniture designs were simple, elegant and graceful. This watercolor

drawing shows his workshops, showrooms and home in New York City. Inside the center building people are examining chairs made by Phyfe.

The room below, from a fashionable New York house, is filled with Duncan Phyfe furniture. The globes indicate a growing interest in trade as American ships sailed the world looking for objects to import. The porcelain bowls are from China and the rug from Central Asia; the cut-glass chandeliers and the material for the curtains and upholstery are from Europe. This type of room was used for entertaining guests and for important family occasions.

Furniture 1800–1820,
The Henry Francis du Pont Winterthur Museum

As the new nation grew wealthier and homes became larger, separate rooms were set aside for dining. Below is a scene of a dinner party which took place in the Boston home of Henry Sargent, who painted this picture. The artist, who was also an army officer, painted a companion piece of a tea party.

The artist emphasized the sense of depth inside the dining room by presenting

The Dinner Party, about 1815–1820, oil, Museum of Fine Arts. Boston, Gift of Mrs. Horatio A. Lamb in memory of Mr. and Mrs. Winthrop Sargent

About 1800–1810,
The Metropolitan Museum of Art,
Gift of the family of
Mr. and Mrs. Andrew Varick Stout,
in their memory, 1881

the scene through the arched doorway in the foreground. The furniture is in the

Hepplewhite and Sheraton styles, named after George Hepplewhite and Thomas

Sheraton, Englishmen who published books of furniture design.

The room is filled with many objects—a clock, wine bottles, lamp, pictures

hanging on the wall, a silver pitcher shaped like an upside-down helmet—all

painted in great detail. An elegant sideboard stands along the wall.

Sideboards were introduced in America at the end of the eighteenth century.

They were useful as both serving tables and cupboards for storage. The sideboard

above was made in the Boston workshop of John and Thomas Seymour.

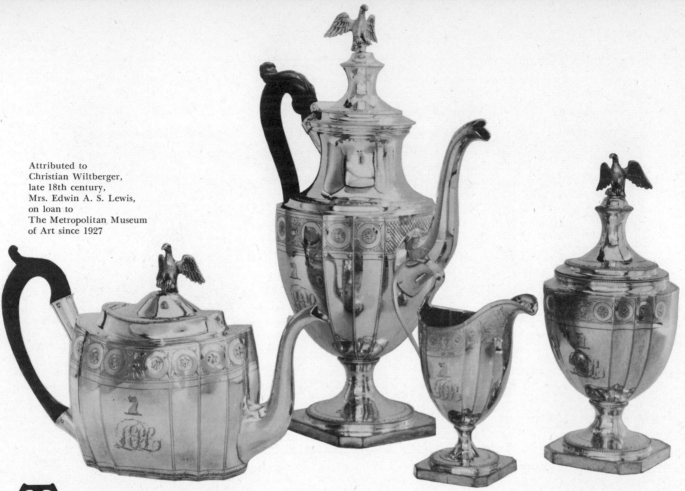

Tea parties were important social events in early America. After the Revolutionary

War many large silver tea sets were made. The silver pieces were often decorated with

eagles, the national symbol of the United States and one of the most popular forms

of decoration in the Federal period. This four-piece tea set was probably a wedding

gift from George Washington to Eleanor Parke Custis.

Fine silver tableware was used for formal dining. The silver sauce boat at right has

a handle in the shape of a serpent and a spout in the form a ram's head. The tea service,

the sauce boat and the large silver presentation vase at far right were all made in

Philadelphia.

The vase was presented to De Witt Clinton, Governor of New York, in celebration

of the opening of the Erie Canal. The design was based on an urn that had been

dug up in Italy at the site of a Roman emperor's villa, or country home. The vase

was made by Thomas Fletcher and Sidney Gardiner. It is decorated with views

of the locks on the canal, barges and surrounding scenery.

The opening of the Erie Canal in 1825 spurred American expansion to the West.

The canal reached across central New York State from Albany

to Buffalo and linked the Hudson River with Lake

Erie. It provided a water passage between

the Great Lakes and the Atlantic Ocean.

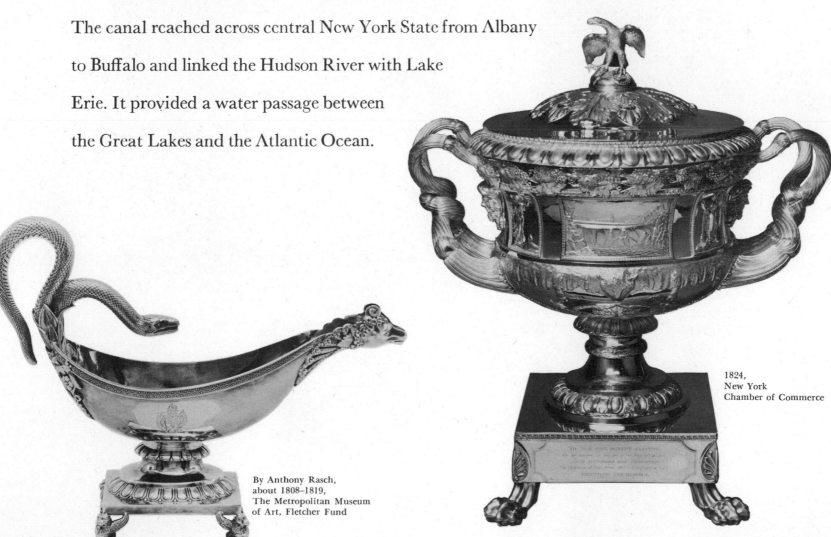

By Anthony Rasch,
about 1808–1819,
The Metropolitan Museum
of Art, Fletcher Fund

1824,
New York
Chamber of Commerce

Early 19th century,
The Metropolitan
Museum of Art,
Gift of
Mrs. Robert W.
de Forest, 1933

In addition to silver and pewter ware, tin utensils were widely used. Tin was cheap, soft and could be easily molded. Traveling peddlers called tinkers carried tin ware far and wide throughout the new states.

Colorful designs were applied to the tin by a process called *japanning,* because it resembled Japanese lacquer ware. The decorations were painted, varnished and baked to make them hard and permanent. At left is a coffee pot made by German settlers in Pennsylvania.

Women stored their hats, collars and bits of lace in bandboxes, which were made of cardboard covered with wallpaper. The wallpaper on this oval bandbox was printed by stenciling. To make a stencil a pattern is cut out in a sheet of heavy paper. The stencil is laid on the surface

About 1820,
The Cooper-Hewitt Museum of
Decorative Arts and Design,
Smithsonian Institution

About 1800–1810,
The Cooper-Hewitt Museum of
Decorative Arts and Design,
Smithsonian Institution

to be decorated and the cutout design is

painted or inked through the openings.

The Federal eagle with outstretched

wings, perched on an urn, is a wallpaper

design from a bandbox. This paper was

printed by woodblocks. A pattern was

carved out of a block of wood. The block

was inked and pressed against the paper

to transfer, or print, the design.

John Frederick Amelung, a German

glassmaker, founded a factory in New

Bremen, Maryland, where this presentation

goblet, or pokal, was made. The pokal

could be used as a drinking cup or a candy

dish. It is engraved with the coat of

arms of the city of Bremen, Germany,

Amelung's home town. It was presented

as a gift from Amelung to his old friends

in Germany.

1788, The Metropolitan Museum
of Art, Rogers Fund, 1928

Mourning Picture for Philo Day,
about 1810,
Abby Aldrich Rockefeller
Folk Art Collection,
Williamsburg, Virginia

In the early nineteenth century many young ladies went to girls' schools, where

fancy needlework and watercolor painting were an important part of their studies.

A popular subject was the mourning picture, a sorrowful tribute to departed loved ones.

This scene in a churchyard was probably copied from an English drawing book. It is

painted with watercolors on silk, and shows tombs, a memorial urn, figures of grieving

ladies and a weeping willow tree. Many mourning pieces were embroidered.

Young girls reviewed their ABC's and at the same time practiced their needlework

by making samplers. The girl who made the sampler at right embroidered her name,

her age, the date, the alphabet and a rhyme, all in cross-stitch. The background cloth

was homespun linen; silk thread was used for the design.

1817, The Cooper-Hewitt Museum
of Decorative Arts and Design,
Smithsonian Institution

ON NEEDLE WORK
With cheerful mind we yield to men,
The higher Honours of the Pen.
The Needle's our great care,
In this we chiefly wish to shine,
How far the arts already mine,
This Sampler does declare.

Ann Wood Aged 8 Years Midsummer 1817

Many early American portrait painters were craftsmen who had never been formally trained in art. Self-taught painters, known as folk artists, often traveled from town to town painting portraits of individuals and

1816, New York State Historical Association, Cooperstown

families. These traveling, or itinerant,

painters usually did not sign their works,

but the artist can sometimes be identified by

the style of the painting.

The unsigned watercolor at left is probably

by George Freeman. Mrs. Elizabeth Fenimore

Cooper is seated in her fine home in Cooperstown,

New York. Tubs of plants are lined up at the

far end of the room; Mrs. Cooper had a "green

thumb." The man standing in the doorway is

James Stewart, known to the Cooper family as

"Governor." Mrs. Cooper was the mother of

Edward and Sarah Rutter,
about 1805, oil,
The Metropolitan Museum of Art,
Gift of Edgar William and
Bernice Chrysler Garbisch, 1965

James Fenimore Cooper, author of many novels about pioneers and Indians.

Joshua Johnston, of Baltimore, was perhaps the first Black American to

become an active portrait painter. Most of his paintings included children.

In the brother and sister portrait above the children are holding strawberries,

a detail often used in Johnston's paintings, which were not signed. The

background of the painting is plain so as not to distract attention from

the children.

Francis Guy was one of the first American genre painters. A genre painting

is a scene of people engaged in everyday activities. Guy painted the neighborhood

in which he lived and used his neighbors as models. His view of Brooklyn in
winter is filled with the activity and charm of life in an early American city.

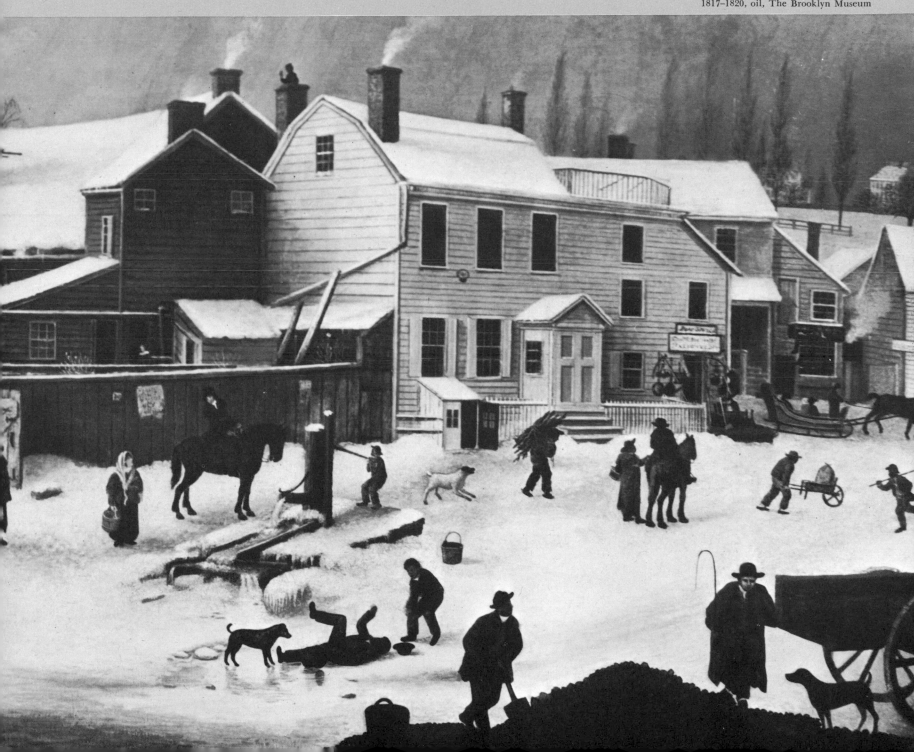

Winter Scene in Brooklyn (detail),
1817–1820, oil, The Brooklyn Museum

Ohio River Landscape, about 1820, oil,
Collection of Mr. and Mrs. Samuel Schwartz

During the early years of the nineteenth century settlers from the East began

to move into the open lands west of the Allegheny Mountains. The painting above,

by an unknown artist, shows two side-wheel steamboats on the Ohio River. Along

the road a horse-drawn carriage moves swiftly. In the distance a plantation house sits on a hill. The artist did not show objects in front of one another. He simply placed more distant objects higher on the canvas.

In the early 1820's artists became inspired by the beauty of the American landscape. Edward Hicks, who had been a sign painter and then a traveling Quaker preacher, was awed by Niagara Falls. He saw this natural wonder as the presence of God in the land. The poem framing the painting expresses his religious feelings.

The Falls of Niagara, 1825, oil, The Metropolitan Museum of Art, Gift of Edgar William and Bernice Chrysler Garbisch, 1962

One of the first artists to explore the Ohio River was John James Audubon. He traveled through the wilderness making detailed drawings of more than a thousand birds. Many had never been seen before by a white man. Some species no longer exist; only the artist's record remains. Above is a watercolor of a turkey hen and her chicks.

During its first fifty years the new nation grew rapidly in size and strength. By 1826 the thirteen original states had been joined by eleven new ones. The young country had already reached the Mississippi River. Before long the new nation would carry its developing art all the way to the Pacific Ocean.